FLOWERS
IN THE
GARDEN

TYLER STEVEN TITTLE

FLOWERS
IN THE
GARDEN

TYLER STEVEN TITTLE

Thistle & Thread Press
Wisconsin, USA
2025

Book Cover by Tyler Steven Tittle
Second printing edition 2025

ISBN: 979-8-89965-836-5

Thistle & Thread Press
Tyler@thistleandthread.org
www.thistleandthread.org

DEDICATION

To my Grandmother,
who taught me to tend soil and sentence.

To my partner,
whose reverence for nature inspired this
collection and gave this book its voice.

Table of Contents

Introduction

This chapbook is a collection of poetic prose rooted in the ancient and ongoing relationship between humans and the natural world. Each piece personifies a plant traditionally used in healing, imagining what that flower might say if it had a voice. Rather than presenting botanical facts or clinical uses, these writings explore the emotional and spiritual essence of each plant; its energy, its history, its archetype.

The idea began with a simple thought: what would the poppy say about pain? What would chamomile whisper to a restless mind? How would motherwort tend to a wounded heart? From that question came an entire field of imagined voices; flowers as guides, as mourners, as midwives, as mirrors. This is nature speaking, not through data, but through metaphor and memory.

These aren't instructional texts. They are stories. They live in the space between poetry and prose. Where feeling takes place over form. They reflect grief, longing, trauma, and resilience, through the lens of the plants that have accompanied us through every era of suffering and survival.

Each piece in the collection stands on its own, yet they are all connected by a common thread: the belief that nature is not silent. That the world we walk through, the fields, forests, gardens, and wild places has its own language, if we are willing to listen.

This work blends literary experimentation with emotional honesty. The writing style is intentionally hybrid: unstructured at times, rhythmic at others, reflecting the natural flow of thought, memory, and the non-linear path of healing. Some entries read like confessions, others like eulogies or prayers. All of them are deeply personal, yet meant to resonate universally.

The goal of this collection is not to explain the properties of herbs, but to embody them. It invites the reader into a garden where each plant is a witness to the human experience. If you come away with a deeper reverence for the earth, a softer place to land inside yourself, or a moment of recognition in the voice of a flower, then the garden has done its work.

Welcome

Poppy

she tends where the broken lie,
in fields stitched shut by gunpowder prayers,
in garden beds once tended by youthful hands.
a beauty cultivated not for the eye,
but for the quiet she brings.

her stems are thin but resolute,
milk-veined and aching with the sap of forgetting.
pierce her green flesh and she weeps white,
not tears, but the sigh of a world unmade.

they called it god's own medicine.
called it laudanum. morphia. syrup of peace.
mother's helper and soldier's ghost.

in dim lantern lit trench hospitals,
she bloomed in the mouths of the dying.
in Victorian parlors,
she curled like incense around velvet curtains
and nervous wrists.

to some she was salvation,
to others, an altar of ruin.
a silence so complete it felt like mercy.
a hand over the mouth of grief.

her petals,
soft as sin,
red as guilt,
fragile as the line between
relief and relapse.

they wrote poems about her after the war,
they still do.
but none that quite get her right.

because how do you name the thing
that heals and haunts you?
that cradles your pain in one palm
and your undoing in the other?

the poppy doesn't speak.
she sings
like a mother crooning lullabies
in the ruins of a burning house.

Chamomile

she is not loud love.
she is the warmth that waits.
the tea that cools in the cup while you cry
in the other room.

no one writes sonnets for the soft things,
but she loves you anyways
in the margins,
in the space between
"I'm fine"
and
"please don't go."

she blooms in overlooked places,
cracks in the stone,
the bend of the road where you stopped
once to catch your breath.
small.
white.
bright.
unremarkable.

until you need her.

and gods,
how she knows when you do.

she doesn't ask what hurt you.
doesn't offer answers.
she just sits with you,
damp and open-handed,
letting your grief steep
until it's drinkable.

you think she's weakness
but you've never seen her survive frost.
never watched her roots hold ground
when the wind roars.

her medicine isn't the cure.
it's the permission,
to rest.
to feel tired without guilt.
to let the ache unfold without shame.

she smells like childhood if it had been safe.
like lullabies sung through locked doors.
like softness that never asks to be earned.

some call her plain.

but you call her when the nights are longest.
when your strength runs out in lowercase sobs.
when your body forgets how to unclench.

and she comes.
she always comes.
barefoot,
blooming,
bearing only this promise:

you don't have to be brave tonight.

Motherwort

she isn't soft,
not in the way you want her to be.
her comfort comes in thorns.
not to harm,
but to keep what needs keeping.
to guard what the world keeps taking.

her name carries a promise
and a grief.
mother.
wort.
the healer of hearts,
even the ones no longer beating.

she blooms where the pain is old.
where the body has learned to lie
about how tired it is.
where grief is no longer loud,
just practiced.
habitual.
swallowed with tea and tight smiles.

she holds you anyway.
not like chamomile,
not gentle.
but steady.
hands beneath your ribs,
cradling the heart you forgot you had.
saying:
i know.
i know how long you've been holding it in.

her medicine is not escape.
it is endurance.
a bitter root.
a taste that reminds you:
you're still here.

she's not the lullaby.
she's the breath between contractions.
she's the woman alone in the bath
with her blood and her body
and no one to thank her.

she is the prayer you mouth
with your fists clenched.
not asking
only surviving.

and when the world tells you
to calm down,
to smile more,
to make yourself smaller,
she blooms taller.
coarse-stemmed.
wild.
green like gall.
green like life.
green like fire.

she doesn't need you to be whole.
just honest.
just present.
just willing to say:

i need a moment.
i need a mother.
i need something that doesn't break
when i lean into it.

and she answers.
without question.
without debt.

Bindweed

he seemed like softness.
white petals, soft coil.
but he wrapped around my ribs
until my breath came
with conditions.
i didn't notice i was suffocating
only that i was being held.

Burdock

you thought you left it behind,
that year,
that wound,
that name,
but it's still caught in your throat.
still burrs in your bloodstream,
still bleeding you in small,
invisible ways.

Nightshade

she never lied.
you **didn't** listen.
you saw purple and thought healing.
you saw berries and thought sweetness.
you kissed her and called it curiosity.
but your mouth still stings
where she said your name
like a grave.

Nettle

you brushed passed her,

thought she was just another green thing.

but she bit back.

left welts where your want touched without asking.

next time,

you'll call it a boundary.

Yarrow

she grows where the wound breaks open
and stays.
not to close it for you,
but to show you how.
white stars,
blood-spattered.
she never flinches.

they say achilles carried her.
tucked her into gashes like a secret.
they say she knew how to speak to blood,
how to slow it, how to seal it,
how to remind it:
you are still needed here.

she doesn't call herself a healer.
she lets your hands do the stitching.
lets your breath steady itself.
she's the kind of help
that never takes the work away from you,
only makes it survivable.

a thousand tiny leaves,
each one a memory of pain
that didn't win.

she promises *return.*
not to what you were,
but to what you've earned.
the version of you that rose
despite.
that learned how to bleed
without *apology.*

she does not bloom for praise.
she blooms because nothing else knows
how to grow on the battlefield
like she does.
because some things
are born to be reminders.

you don't harvest her.
you meet her.
on your feet.
on your own terms.
and when you do,
you know you're ready
to walk out of the garden.

Afterward

If you have made it this far, then you already understand: every plant has a voice. Some whisper, some scream, some simply wait for you to notice them. May this be your permission to begin listening. To speak back. The next time you pass a tree, a roadside weed, a bloom too stubborn to die: pause. Ask what it knows. Ask what it remembers. Let the world become a conversation again, not a conquest. There is language in the wild, and it's been waiting for you.

Thank you for spending time in this garden. For pausing long enough to notice the voices blooming beneath the surface. Your presence here matters, not just to me, but to the stories that might have gone unheard without you.

By supporting this chapbook, you've uplifted the work of an independent writer and a growing press built on roots, resilience, and the belief that even the quietest of voices deserve space to grow.

As you close these pages, I invite you to open your world a little wider. Let every thing you pass remind you: you are part of this living, breathing conversation. And it's only just begun.